24

N

WASHOE COUNTY LIBRARY

3 1235 02884 0564

J
940
.5425
HOO
2003

## DATE DUE

| | | |
|---|---|---|
| APR 2 6 2004 | | |
| AUG 1 0 2004 | | |
| JUN 0 9 2005 | | |
| | | |
| | | |
| | | |
| | | |
| | | |
| | | |
| | | |
| | | |
| | | |
| | | |
| | | |
| GAYLORD | | PRINTED IN U.S.A. |

D1123776

No Longer Property Of
Washoe County Library

NORTH VALLEYS
LIBRARY

# DAYS THAT SHOOK THE WORLD
## AUGUST 6, 1945

## HIROSHIMA

# DAYS THAT SHOOK THE WORLD

# HIROSHIMA

## AUGUST 6, 1945

### Jason Hook

**RAINTREE**
**STECK-VAUGHN**
**PUBLISHERS**

A Harcourt Company

Austin   New York
www.raintreesteckvaughn.com

# DAYS THAT SHOOK THE WORLD

Assassination in Sarajevo
The Chernobyl Disaster
D-Day
The Dream of Martin Luther King
The Fall of the Berlin Wall

Hiroshima
The Kennedy Assassination
The Moon Landing
Pearl Harbor
The Wall Street Crash

© Copyright 2003, text, Steck-Vaughn Company

All rights reserved. No part of this book may be reproduced or utilized in any form or by any means, electronic or mechanical, including photocopying, recording, or by any information storage and retrieval system, without permission in writing from the Publishers. Inquiries should be addressed to: Copyright Permissions, Steck-Vaughn Company, P.O. Box 26015, Austin, TX 78755

Published by Raintree Steck-Vaughn Publishers,
an imprint of Steck-Vaughn Company

**Library of Congress Cataloging-in-Publication Data is available upon request.**

ISBN 0-7398-5234-5

Printed in Italy. Bound in the United States.

1  2  3  4  5  6  7  8  9  0  LB  06  05  04  03  02

### Picture Acknowledgments:

Cover picture: A mushroom cloud rises following the test explosion of an atomic bomb over Bikini Atoll in 1954 (Corbis).
Title page picture: The immense force of the Hiroshima nuclear blast flattened many buildings and twisted others beyond recognition (Corbis/Charles Rosecrans).

We are grateful to the following for permission to reproduce photographs: Associated Press 28, 43 (Shizuo Kambayashi); Bettmann/Corbis 7 left, 8, 13, 15, 19, 21, 25, 27, 31, 37, 42; Camera Press Ltd 12 (Imperial War Museum), 40; Corbis 6, 9, 10, 14, 16 top, 16 bottom (Lucien Aigner), 17, 18, 22, 24, 29 left (Lt Wayne Miller), 29 right (Charles Rosecrans), 30, 33, 34, 35 bottom (Dennis Degnan), 41; Hulton-Deutsch Collection/Corbis 35 top, 36; Topham 7 right, 20, 23, 26, 32, 38. 39, 46.

# CONTENTS

The crew of the B-29 bomber Enola Gay at North Field air base in the early hours of August 6, 1945.

" If only I had known, I would have become a watchmaker. "

*Albert Einstein, on his part in developing the atomic bomb.*

IN THE EARLY HOURS of Monday, August 6, 1945, a strange scene unfolded on a tiny island in the middle of the Pacific Ocean. Floodlights lit up a huddle of nearly 100 people. There were film crews, photographers, journalists, scientists, soldiers, and government agents. All gathered on a runway beneath an enormous silver American B-29 Superfortress bomber. The plane's 12 crewmen, wearing overalls and baseball caps, blinked into the cameras. Their mission was so secret that most of them did not know its exact nature.

By August 1945, the Pacific had become the main battleground of World War II. The Allies, led by Great Britain, the United States, and the Soviet Union, had defeated Nazi Germany. But Germany's ally, Japan, still refused to surrender. American forces had recaptured most of the islands invaded by Japan earlier in the war. Tinian, one of the Mariana Islands some 1,429 miles (2,300 km) southeast of Japan, was now home to the United States' North Field air base. From here, American B-29s—the biggest bombers in the world—took off night after night to bomb Japan.

But the flight on August 6 was different. Special Bombing Mission No. 13 was the first to be undertaken by the mysterious 509th Composite Group. For almost a year, this group's airmen had been exempt from the duties of other bombing crews. They had made a few flights to drop big, round, orange bombs known as "pumpkins," but even these flights had not been recorded. It was almost as if the 509th did not exist.

The day before the attack on Hiroshima, the Enola Gay was positioned over a special pit. The atomic bomb Little Boy was winched up from this pit into the plane's bomb-bay.

At 2:45 A.M., the bomber rumbled down the runway with the leader of the 509th, Colonel Paul Tibbets, at the controls. Only the previous day, he had ordered a signwriter to paint the plane with the name Enola Gay—after his mother, who had first encouraged him to fly. Even as the paint dried, the bomber's secret cargo was being winched into position behind the cover of a canvas screen.

Carrying more than 6,600 gallons (25,000 L) of fuel and its secret cargo, the Enola Gay was massively overloaded. The end of the North Field runway was a sheer drop into the sea and, as it drew nearer, Tibbets was still short of the speed needed to get the plane off the ground. Of the crew, only Tibbets and three others knew the full danger of this takeoff. The Enola Gay was carrying a bomb that weighed over four tons. Known as Little Boy, the bomb was the product of a $2 billion research program. It was the most destructive weapon ever created. At the last second, Tibbets eased back the controls and the silver bomber lumbered into the air.

The day of the world's first atomic bomb attack had begun.

A model of Little Boy, the first atomic bomb to be used in war.

## A Moment in Time

As the Enola Gay struggles into the air, 1,553 miles (2,500 km) away the "all-clear" siren has just sounded in the Japanese city of Hiroshima. People are hurrying from air-raid shelters back to their homes. The Japanese call the B-29 bomber "B-San," which means Mr. B. They can even buy recordings of B-San's engines, so that they learn to recognize the sound of the bomber's approach. For the last year, observers in Hiroshima have watched B-San pass overhead, but no B-29 has ever dropped its bombs on the city. Enola Gay will be the first and last.

The American battleships *West Virginia* and *Tennessee* ablaze, following the Japanese attack at Pearl Harbor.

THE EVENTS LEADING UP TO the flight of the Enola Gay can be traced back to another day that shook the world. On the morning of Sunday, December 7, 1941, the U.S. Pacific Fleet lay peacefully at anchor in Pearl Harbor, on the Hawaiian island of Oahu. Neither the United States nor Japan had yet entered World War II, but the previous year Japan had formed an alliance with Germany and Italy. Just before 8:00 A.M., Japanese warplanes swept over the horizon in such numbers that they looked like a swarm of bees. Moored in neat rows, the American ships were sitting

ducks. The water in Pearl Harbor erupted with the explosions of bombs and torpedoes. Taking the Americans completely by surprise, the Japanese planes destroyed or damaged 18 ships at anchor and 347 aircraft on the ground. More than 2,400 Americans were killed, and more than 1,000 wounded.

The American people were horrified by the attack, which came before any clear declaration of war. In fact, at the same moment that Japanese planes were bombing Pearl Harbor, officials from the United

*...we here highly resolve that these dead shall not have died in vain...*

**REMEMBER DEC. 7th!**

Many American propaganda posters referred to the attack on Pearl Harbor.

population had enabled its government to conscript a huge army, and develop the world's third-largest navy. The government was controlled by ambitious army officers who wished to carve out a massive empire in Southeast Asia. Only the U.S. Pacific Fleet was powerful enough to prevent them—so Japan blew it out of the water at Pearl Harbor.

The attack was a dramatic military victory for Japan, but would prove to be a long-term disaster. It stirred a desire for revenge in the United States, which at this time was the only nation capable of standing up to Japan. President Franklin D. Roosevelt called December 7, 1941 "a date that will live in infamy," expressing the anger Americans felt at the surprise attack. The United States now entered World War II on the side of the Allies, declaring war on Japan, Germany, and Italy. The slogans "Remember Pearl Harbor!" and "Remember December 7th" soon appeared on postcards, pencils, and pillowcases. They are slogans that should not be forgotten when considering the decision made more than three years later to drop an atomic bomb on Hiroshima.

States and Japan were meeting in Washington D.C. to discuss their differences. In 1937, Japanese troops had invaded China, raping and massacring thousands of people in Nanking. In July 1941, they had attacked French Indo-China (now Vietnam, Laos, and Cambodia). The United States, wishing to protect its own interests in Southeast Asia, China, and the Philippines, had responded by stopping supplies of oil from reaching Japan.

Today, it is difficult to imagine Japan attacking the United States, but in December 1941 the world was very different. With a population of more than 70 million, Japan was the most crowded nation on earth—and did not have enough raw materials to support its people. Japan's leaders believed it was vital to capture regions such as the Dutch East Indies that could supply resources like oil. Japan's teeming

## Emperor Hirohito (1901–1989)

Japan's supreme ruler, Emperor Hirohito, was considered a sacred being. When he took the throne on Christmas Day 1926, he became the 124th emperor in an unbroken line dating back 2,600 years. His unusual role was described as "above the clouds"—he was higher than everything, and too high to become involved in politics. So, although Hirohito personally opposed the war, he had to remain silent and give his blessing to the decisions of his ministers.

Thousands of captured American troops in the Philippines in April 1942, during the ordeal that became known as the Bataan Death March.

## A Prisoner's View

" More and more people see the horror of Hiroshima... out of context. They tend to see it increasingly as an act of history in which we alone were the villains. I have been amazed to observe how in some extraordinary kind of way my own Japanese friends do not seem to feel that they had done anything themselves to provoke us into inflicting Hiroshima... on them, and how strangely uncurious they are about their own part in the war. "

*Laurens Van Der Post in* Night of the New Moon. *The author was held prisoner in a Japanese camp during World War II.*

THE JAPANESE ATTACK ON Pearl Harbor was part of a carefully laid plan. With the U.S. Navy crippled, Japan would invade Southeast Asia—occupying a "Southern Resources Area" from which vital materials could be transported to Japan to sustain the war effort. At the same time, troops would occupy the islands that were dotted across the western Pacific. These islands would provide a defensive buffer against American retaliation. By defending them fiercely and harassing the U.S. Navy in the Pacific, Japan hoped to force a truce that would leave the conquered territories under its control.

From December 1941 to May 1942, Japanese forces swept all before them. American pride was further dented by defeat in the Philippines. British troops were overrun in Hong Kong, Malaya, Burma, and Singapore, and the Dutch were driven from the East Indies (now Indonesia). In only six months, Japan conquered nearly 1 million square miles (1.5 million sq km) of land, assumed rule over 150 million new people, and captured nearly half-a-million prisoners of war.

Japan had a very different culture from its enemies, and Japanese soldiers held beliefs that now seem strange amid the tanks and guns of modern warfare. As schoolchildren, they had learned of their sacred duty to die for the emperor, who was said to embody the spiritual essence of Japan. When the clouds had parted over Pearl Harbor as the Japanese planes approached, the pilots believed it was a sign of divine favor.

Hardened by a brutal training regime, Japanese soldiers followed the *Bushido* code of the ancient Samurai warriors of Japan. According to this code, surrender was cowardly and shameful. Many Japanese soldiers felt contempt for the thousands of Allied troops who surrendered to them. Instead of receiving fair treatment, as agreed in the Geneva Convention, prisoners of war under the Japanese faced a brutal captivity. Shelter, food, and medicine were scarce, and tropical diseases such as malaria were rife. Sick and starving prisoners were forced to work for their Japanese captors. Some 12,000 died constructing the Burma–Thailand railway through mountains and jungle.

On one infamous occasion, more than 70,000 exhausted American and Filipino troops captured at Bataan in the Philippines were made to walk 62 miles (100 km) to their designated prison camp. At least 7,000 died on what became known as the Bataan Death March. Soldiers were randomly beaten, bayoneted, or beheaded, and some were forced to bury their comrades alive. Accounts of experiences such as this shaped American attitudes toward their Japanese enemies.

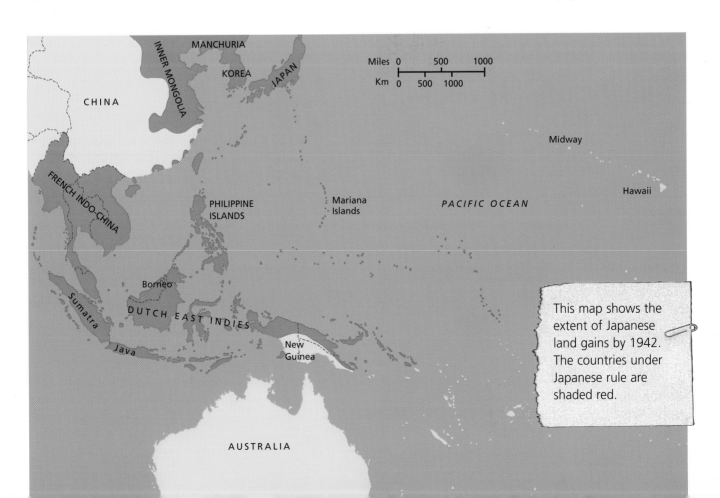

This map shows the extent of Japanese land gains by 1942. The countries under Japanese rule are shaded red.

In the spring of 1945, U.S. Marines advancing across Okinawa spare a glance at the Japanese dead.

O**N APRIL 1, 1945, U.S. Marines landed on the Japanese-held island of Okinawa, only 342 miles (550 km) from Japan. It was the culmination of an extraordinary three-year campaign by the Allies to drive the Japanese back across the Pacific.

In June 1942, U.S. aircraft carriers defeated a Japanese fleet attacking Midway Island, north of Hawaii. The tide of the war was beginning to turn. Gradually, Allied ships won control of the seas. In October 1944, the Japanese navy was destroyed in the biggest naval conflict in history: the Battle of Leyte Gulf. Supported by the navy, U.S. troops began to "island-hop"—fighting bloody battles to recapture the islands dotted across the vastness of the Pacific and using them as stepping stones to edge ever closer to Japan. At the same time, the U.S. war machine grew. American factories built 17 new aircraft carriers before the war's end, and in 1944 they were producing one aircraft every five minutes. Over half-a-million troops and 1,300 ships were employed in the invasion of Okinawa, and American ships used more oil at Okinawa than Japan had imported during the whole of the previous year.

The Japanese were running short of ships, planes, and trained pilots. They adopted desperate tactics, and began launching kamikaze attacks. The kamikazes were suicide bombers whose mission was to fly planes packed with explosives into American ships. At Okinawa, 1,465 kamikaze pilots sacrificed their lives, damaging 120 Allied ships of which 29 sank. Perhaps the most amazing kamikaze was the world's biggest battleship *Yamato*, which the Japanese leaders sent on a one-way suicide mission to attack the American fleet at Okinawa. It was sunk by American planes, with the loss of 3,000 Japanese lives.

The land battle at Okinawa also revealed Japan's ancient Bushido tradition of no surrender. Cornered soldiers mounted suicidal *banzai* charges, screaming "Tenno heika banzai!" ("Long live the emperor!") Their commanding officer committed suicide by disemboweling himself, in a sacred ritual known as *seppuku*, to avoid the disgrace of defeat.

Some 110,000 defenders of Okinawa fought to the death. American losses were also heavy, with more than 12,000 dead and 40,000 wounded.

The fanatical way in which the Japanese fought for islands like Okinawa had three effects. It made the Americans think of the "Jap" as an alien, inhuman enemy. It illustrated how fiercely the Japanese would defend their homeland. And it suggested that an invasion of Japan itself would involve terrible Allied casualties. Such thoughts would make it easier to wave the Enola Gay on her way.

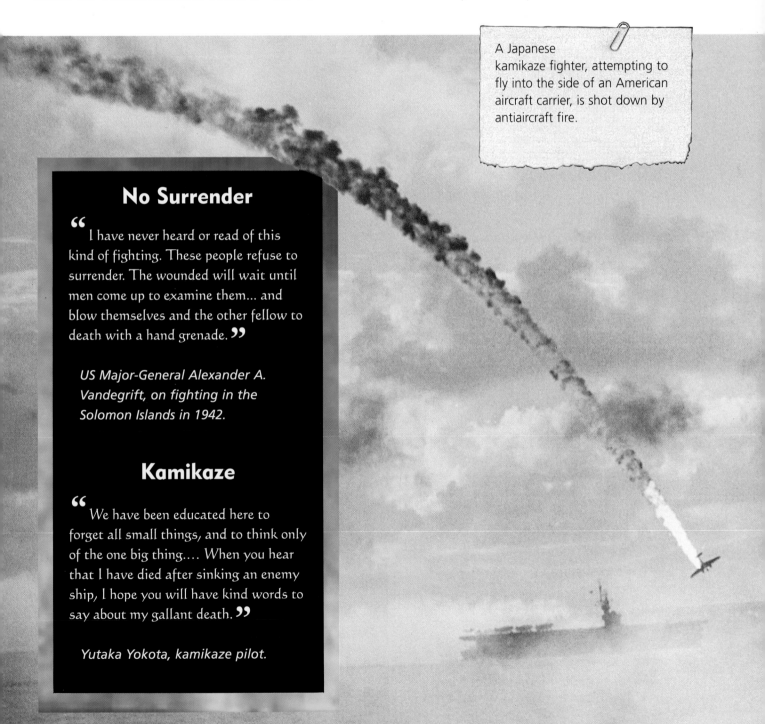

A Japanese kamikaze fighter, attempting to fly into the side of an American aircraft carrier, is shot down by antiaircraft fire.

## No Surrender

" I have never heard or read of this kind of fighting. These people refuse to surrender. The wounded will wait until men come up to examine them... and blow themselves and the other fellow to death with a hand grenade. "

*US Major-General Alexander A. Vandegrift, on fighting in the Solomon Islands in 1942.*

## Kamikaze

" We have been educated here to forget all small things, and to think only of the one big thing.... When you hear that I have died after sinking an enemy ship, I hope you will have kind words to say about my gallant death. "

*Yutaka Yokota, kamikaze pilot.*

A cascade of incendiary bombs falls from American B-29 bombers during one of the "firestorm" raids that devastated Japan in the spring and summer of 1945.

DURING THE WAR, THE United States had been developing the Boeing B-29 Superfortress, the giant aircraft that would one day drop the world's first atomic bomb. The B-29 was the largest bomber ever built, with a wingspan of 141 feet (43 m). It was hurried into service by test pilots, including one Colonel Paul Tibbets.

On June 15, 1944, the first B-29s raided Japan from bases in China. On the same day, U.S. Marines staged bloody landings on the beaches of Saipan in the Marianas. The two events were strangely connected— the Marianas would provide bases close enough to Japan for the B-29s to have a major impact on the war. Four months later, a B-29 named Joltin' Josie became the first to land on Saipan. The Marianas

soon became crisscrossed with enormous runways. By November, the giant, silver bombers were pounding Japan's cities and factories.

Early in 1945, Major-General Curtis LeMay took charge of the bombing campaign in the Marianas. He introduced a new type of bombing, sending the B-29s in low at night to scatter thousands of incendiary bombs. The population of Japan was the most crowded in the world, with people living in densely packed cities crammed with paper-and-wood houses. The incendiaries would set these houses ablaze. On the night of March 9, 1945, more than 300 B-29s swarmed from the Marianas to drop over 2,000 tons of incendiary bombs on Tokyo. The bombs created a huge firestorm, whipping up a hurricane and making the city's canals boil. A quarter of Tokyo was turned to ashes, and more than 80,000 civilians perished.

In the following months, LeMay's "firestorm" raids devastated Japan's cities. By this stage in the war there were so few aircraft defending Japan that the Americans could announce their targets in advance. They even dropped leaflets warning civilians of their impending doom, to weaken Japanese morale. The bombing resulted in a staggering number of casualties, but LeMay felt the attacks were justified. He argued that it would be immoral to use less force, illustrating his point with the story of a man who cut off his dog's tail a bit at a time so that it would hurt less.

By August 1945, the bombing had made 8 million Japanese people homeless, and LeMay was running out of targets. But the cities of Hiroshima, Nagasaki, Kokuta, and Niigata remained untouched. The U.S. War Department had special plans for them. As well as developing the B-29, the United States had been working on a weapon that would allow the troublesome Japanese "tail" to be cut off with one brutal blow.

An aerial photograph of Tokyo in 1945. The American bombing raids had reduced Japan's capital city to rubble.

## Casualties of War

" You're going to kill an awful lot of civilians. Thousands and thousands. But if you don't destroy the Japanese industry, we're going to have to invade Japan. And how many Americans will be killed in an invasion of Japan? Five hundred thousand seems to be the lowest estimate. Some say a million. "

" I'll tell you what war is about, you've got to kill people, and when you've killed enough, they stop fighting. "

*Major-General Curtis LeMay (1906–1990).*

```
                                    Albert Einstein
                                    Old Grove Rd.
                                    Nassau Point
                                    Peconic, Long Island

                                    August 2nd, 1939

F.D. Roosevelt,
President of the United States,
White House
Washington, D.C.

Sir:

     Some recent work by E.Fermi and L. Szilard, which has been com-
municated to me in manuscript, leads me to expect that the element uran-
ium may be turned into a new and important source of energy in the im-
mediate future. Certain aspects of the situation which has arisen seem
to call for watchfulness and, if necessary, quick action on the part
of the Administration. I believe therefore that it is my duty to bring
to your attention the following facts and recommendations:

     In the course of the last four months it has been made probable -
through the work of Joliot in France as well as Fermi and Szilard in
America - that it may become possible to set up a nuclear chain reaction
'n a large mass
```

Einstein wrote his letter to President Roosevelt on August 2, 1939, a month before Germany invaded Poland.

**W**ORLD WAR II progressed alongside a race to build the weapon that would end it. On December 8, 1938, the German scientist Otto Hahn carried out an experiment in which uranium atoms were bombarded with particles called neutrons, and succeeded in splitting a uranium atom. This process—known as fission—released the enormous energy that held the atom's particles together. The discovery would lead to the invention of the world's most destructive weapon, and it was made in Nazi Germany on the eve of history's most destructive war.

Adolf Hitler's persecution of the Jewish population in Europe produced an ironic side effect. It forced many scientists to flee abroad—and supplied the Allies with teams of brilliant minds to develop Hahn's research. Among them was the Hungarian physicist Leo Szilard, who quickly recognized the destructive potential of fission. Szilard demonstrated that a chain reaction—

where the splitting of one atom causes the splitting of others—could release enough energy to create a huge explosion.

The most renowned German refugee of all was Albert Einstein, who had emigrated to the United States in 1933 after Hitler's rise to power. In 1905, Einstein had reasoned that atoms were held together by forces containing enormous energy. Now he helped Szilard to warn the American government of what could be achieved by releasing this energy. On August 2, 1939, Einstein wrote a letter to President Roosevelt, describing the possibility of creating an atomic bomb and urging the United States to build one before the Nazis did. A month later, Germany invaded Poland. World War II and the race to build the atomic bomb had begun simultaneously.

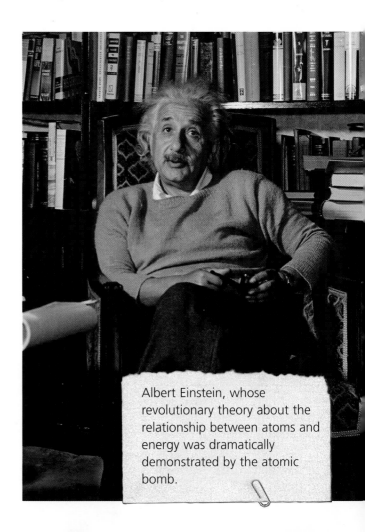

Albert Einstein, whose revolutionary theory about the relationship between atoms and energy was dramatically demonstrated by the atomic bomb.

The Italian genius Enrico Fermi. He received the Nobel Prize for physics on the eve of World War II, then constructed the world's first atomic reactor.

Allied scientists discovered that uranium contained two substances suitable for fission, and they named these U-235 and plutonium. Under the command of Brigadier-General Leslie Groves, the top-secret Manhattan Project was launched to develop these substances into an atomic bomb. It would require billions of dollars, monstrous new machines, and over 600,000 workers. The project was given impetus by the Austrian scientist, Otto Frisch, who had been working in Britain on methods for using fission to make a bomb.

The world's first atomic reactor was created by Italian genius Enrico Fermi—in a squash court beneath the University of Chicago football stadium! He constructed an "atomic pile" of 45,000 graphite bricks, into which 45 tons of uranium was loaded. It was believed that such a quantity of uranium would create its own chain reaction. At 3:25 P.M. on December 2, 1942, Fermi removed the control rods from his reactor. Measuring instruments began to rattle in a constant drumroll, announcing the release of atomic energy. Scientists driven from Europe by Hitler had led the United States into the atomic age. One American said of Fermi's achievement, "The Italian navigator has landed in the New World."

## The Prediction

"This new phenomenon would also lead to the construction of bombs, and it is conceivable—though much less certain—that extremely powerful bombs of a new type may thus be constructed. A single bomb of this type, carried by boat and exploded in a port, might very well destroy the whole port together with some of the surrounding territory. "

*From Albert Einstein's letter to President Roosevelt, 1939.*

## A Great Mistake

"I made one great mistake in my life, when I signed the letter to President Roosevelt. "

*Albert Einstein, regretting his part in the creation of the atomic bomb.*

The world's first atomic bomb explodes at Alamogordo, New Mexico, on July 16, 1945.

ON DECEMBER 7, 1942, exactly one year after the raid on Pearl Harbor, agents from the Manhattan Project closed down the Los Alamos Ranch School in the middle of the New Mexico desert. A laboratory was built in its place. Here, 100 brilliant scientists gathered, including Fermi and Niels Bohr, the Dane who had discovered U-235. They were led by 38-year-old lecturer Dr. J. Robert Oppenheimer, who had reacted to the discovery of fission by drawing a bomb on his blackboard at Berkeley, California.

Believing they were engaged in a deadly race against Nazi scientists, Oppenheimer's team produced two designs for an atomic bomb. The first was like a gun, in which a "bullet" of U-235 was fired into a target of the same material. The meeting of the two pieces created a chain reaction of splitting atoms. A uranium bomb of this design, named Little Boy, would be dropped on Hiroshima. The second design was a ball of plutonium surrounded by explosives. These would create shock waves that squeezed the plutonium tighter, again creating a chain reaction. A plutonium bomb of this type, named Fat Man, would be the first atomic bomb ever tested. A plutonium bomb would also be dropped on the Japanese city of Nagasaki.

On Monday, July 16, 1945, a test—codenamed Trinity—revealed the fruits of the Los Alamos labors. At 5:00 A.M., searchlights illuminated a 98-foot (30-m)-high steel tower at the Alamogordo bombing range in an isolated desert known, fittingly, as the Journey of Death. In a steel shed at the tower's top sat the Fat

Robert Oppenheimer (center) leans forward to inspect all that remains of the tower that held the Fat Man. In uniform at his side is General Groves, leader of the Manhattan Project.

Man. It contained a solid plutonium core the size of a tennis ball. Nobody knew how powerful the bomb might be. Fermi had taken bets on whether it would ignite the atmosphere and consume the entire world!

At 5:10 A.M., the countdown began. On a hill 18.6 miles (30 km) from the Fat Man, scientists who had assembled to watch the test put on sunglasses and suntan lotion. In a bunker only 5 miles (8 km) from the bomb, Oppenheimer—exhausted and racked by nerves—clung to a post for support.

At 5:30 A.M., just before dawn, the explosives fired. They squeezed Fat Man's core of uranium to the size of a squash ball, and the dark sky was torn open by a flash so blinding it could have been seen from the planet Venus. An immense fireball blossomed into the sky, contorting itself into a brilliant purple mushroom cloud 5.6 miles (9 km) high. Heat surged over the stunned observers, one of whom said later, "It was like opening a hot oven, with the sun coming out like a sunrise."

Oppenheimer whispered a line from Hindu scripture, "Now I am become Death, the shatterer of worlds." The atomic age had dawned.

## A Moment in Time

At 5:30 A.M., the exploding Fat Man evaporates the tower beneath it. The sand below is turned to green glass by the heat. Five miles (8 km) from the blast, observers are flattened by the shock wave. Ten miles (16 km) away, a drunken chef is blinded by the flash, and vows never to drink again. Nearly 187 miles (300 km) away at Gallup, New Mexico, windows suddenly shatter. On the Arizona border, a woman asks herself a question: "Why has the sun risen twice this morning?"

The leaders of the Allies (left to right), Churchill, Truman, and Stalin, at Potsdam, Germany, in July 1945.

As Oppenheimer's scientists made their final preparations for the Trinity test, Harry S. Truman, the new American president, arrived in Potsdam, near Berlin, for a conference with British prime minister Winston Churchill and Soviet leader Joseph Stalin. Nazi Germany had surrendered to the Allies two months earlier, and Truman now planned to persuade Stalin to join the war against Japan.

The following afternoon, however, Truman received a coded message from Washington, "Operated on this morning. Diagnosis not yet complete but results seem satisfactory." It meant the Fat Man had been a success—the Manhattan Project had found a way for the United States to win the war on its own. Suddenly, Truman did not need Stalin's help, in fact the president now wished to defeat Japan before troops from the Soviet Union could become involved.

On July 26, 1945, Truman and Churchill (after whom the Fat Man had been named) issued the Potsdam Proclamation, outlining the conditions for a Japanese surrender. It ended: "We call upon the government of Japan to proclaim now the unconditional surrender of all Japanese armed forces…. The alternative for Japan is prompt and utter destruction."

By now, Japan's air and sea defenses had been destroyed, her cities had been reduced to rubble, and her people were starving. Some of her officials had expressed a willingness to surrender, but with one condition—Emperor Hirohito, spirit of Japan's ancient honor, must be allowed to keep his throne. The proclamation, though, made no mention of the emperor or a new type of bomb. Kantaro Suzuki, the Japanese prime minister, rejected it.

Japan had 28 million civilians willing to fight to the death, with pitchforks and bamboo spears, for the sake of their emperor. Having seen the ferocious defense of islands such as Okinawa, some American generals estimated that an invasion of Japan might cost a half-a-million American lives. But Truman now had an alternative, a weapon that meant he could demand surrender without conditions, which meant that an invasion might not be necessary, and that had cost his country over $2 billion to create.

On the same day that the Potsdam Proclamation was made, the cruiser USS *Indianapolis* arrived at Tinian in the Marianas. On board were two mysterious passengers with a strange cargo—a wooden crate and an enormously heavy bucket— that they had transported chained to the floor of their cabin. It was rumored among the ship's crew that the bucket was full of gold to bribe Japan into surrender. In fact, it contained a bullet of U-235 for use in the Manhattan Project's latest creation— an atomic bomb, named Little Boy after the late President Roosevelt.

When Japan rejected the Potsdam Proclamation, Truman gave the order: "Release when ready!"

## Harry S. Truman (1884–1972)

Harry S. Truman had not sought to be president. The office was thrust upon him when President Franklin D. Roosevelt died of a brain hemorrhage on April 12, 1945. The presidency came with an added burden. Such was the secrecy surrounding the Manhattan Project that Truman, the former vice-president, did not find out about the atomic bomb until the day he became president. But Truman had no hesitation in using the bomb, noting in his diary at Potsdam: "It seems to be the most terrible thing ever discovered, but it can be made the most useful."

The USS *Indianapolis* delivered parts of the atomic bomb to Tinian. Three days after leaving Tinian, she was sunk by a Japanese submarine.

This photograph captures the historic moment when the Enola Gay took off to begin its flight to Hiroshima.

COLONEL PAUL TIBBETS BELIEVED that August 6, 1945 was going to be the day that would end the war. In the first minutes after midnight he briefed his crew, and then joined them for a breakfast of ham, eggs, and pineapple fritters.

**1:37 A.M.** (Tinian time) Three B-29s took off from North Field to check the weather over Japan. The preferred target for the Enola Gay was a city on the main Japanese island of Honshu, which contained military headquarters, factories, and workers' homes. It had been spared any previous bombing, so Little Boy's devastation would show up clearly. The name of the city was Hiroshima.

**2:45 A.M.** The Enola Gay lumbered into the air, followed by two B-29s loaded with cameras and measuring devices.

**3:00 A.M.** Captain William Parsons, the Manhattan Project officer who was responsible for looking after the bomb, clambered down into the Enola Gay's belly. It had been considered too dangerous for the plane to take off with Little Boy fully assembled. Now, at 6,562 feet

(2,000 m) and with the bomb hanging by a single hook, Parsons gently inserted the explosive charges.

(All the following times are those in Hiroshima, where clocks were an hour behind Tinian time.)

**6:30 A.M.** Parsons replaced three green plugs in the bomb with red ones. Little Boy was now live. Tibbets' co-pilot, Captain Robert Lewis, noted, "I had a feeling the bomb had a life of its own now that had nothing to do with us." As the Enola Gay flew into the rising sun, Tibbets shared a secret with his crew: "We are carrying the world's first atomic bomb."

**7:24 A.M.** One of the weather planes reported that there were no clouds over Hiroshima. The city's last hope of salvation was gone.

**8:12 A.M.** The Enola Gay reached "IP," the Initial Point of the bombing run. Major Thomas Ferebee, the bombardier, looked down into the sights he would use to aim Little Boy at its target. The crew pulled on sun-goggles to protect their eyes from the glare of the atom bomb's imminent explosion.

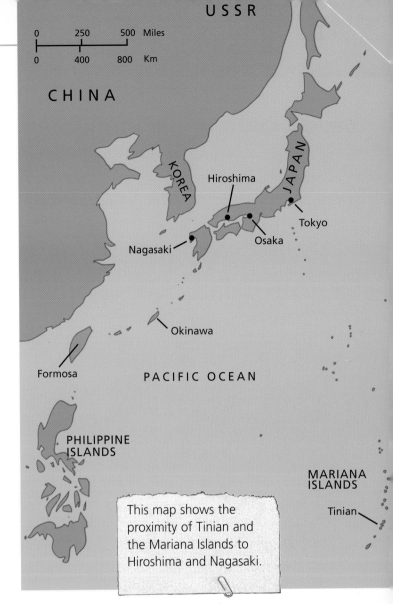

This map shows the proximity of Tinian and the Mariana Islands to Hiroshima and Nagasaki.

**8:14 A.M.** Ferebee had studied photographs of Hiroshima. Now he stared down as the city's landmarks scrolled past, 5.6 miles (9 km) below him. He was looking for the Aioi Bridge, which formed a perfect "T" where it spanned the Ota River in the center of Hiroshima. A radio tone began droning in the crew's ears to warn them that the bomb was about to be dropped. It would last until the bomb was released.

**8:15 A.M.** The bridge appeared in Ferebee's sights. The radio tone ceased. The doors in the Enola Gay's belly swung open. Ferebee shouted: "Bomb away!"

Little Boy was plummeting toward Hiroshima.

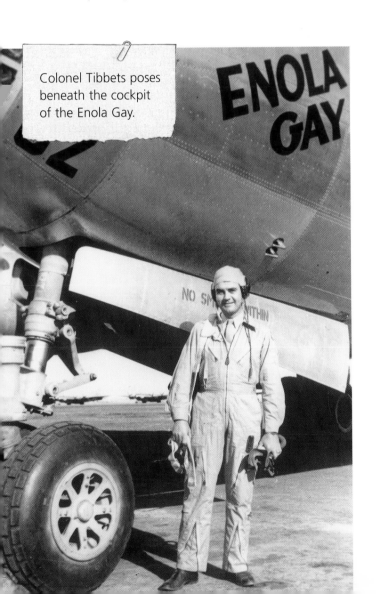

Colonel Tibbets poses beneath the cockpit of the Enola Gay.

## A Moment in Time

As Tibbets' crewmen follow the procedures of their mission, thousands of feet beneath them the Japanese are also performing their duties. At 6:00 A.M., radar operators lock on to the Enola Gay. Just after 7:00 A.M., wardens sound an air-raid siren when the B-29 weather plane, called Straight Flush, is spotted over Hiroshima. At 8:13 A.M., observers in a lookout station east of Hiroshima sight the Enola Gay. They report its approach, but can have no notion of what the bomber is carrying.

Moments after Little Boy explodes over Hiroshima, an enormous mushroom cloud rises above the devastated city.

THE BOMB FALLING OUT of the sky over Hiroshima measured 9.8 feet (3 m) from tip to tail, and weighed over four tons. Its black steel casing was scrawled with graffiti taunting the enemy. The *Indianapolis*, which had delivered Little Boy to Tinian, had been sunk shortly afterward by a Japanese submarine. Five hundred American lives had been lost, and one message scrawled on the bomb read: "Greetings to the Emperor from the men of the *Indianapolis*."

Little Boy was very different from the Fat Man, the plutonium bomb demonstrated at Alamogordo. A bomb like Little Boy, which worked by firing two pieces of U-235 together, had never been tested. There was no guarantee that it would even explode.

**8:15 A.M.** As it was released from the plane, the first of three switches inside the bomb closed. Tibbets swung the Enola Gay into a violent dive to the right, so that the plane would avoid being caught in the blast. When Little Boy had descended to 4,921 feet (1,500 m) from the ground, a second switch was triggered.

## A Moment in Time

It is a warm, still morning in Hiroshima, and people are going about their everyday lives. Many are at work. Dr. Terufumi Sasaki, a 25-year-old surgeon, strides through the Red Cross Hospital. In the downtown area, a schoolgirl who has joined thousands of others looks up as her teacher points at "B-San." Near Hiroshima Castle, a soldier joining the vast ranks exercising on a parade ground stares at a blindfolded prisoner of war—a captured American bomber pilot. Some people, such as 5-year-old Myeko Nakamura, are asleep in their homes. At 8:16 A.M., they are illuminated by a blinding white flash—it is as though a huge photograph is being taken of their city.

An aerial reconnaissance photograph of the area destroyed by the bomb. The numbers refer to military and industrial targets.

**INDEX**

A·P INDICATES AIMING POINT

| | | | | | |
|---|---|---|---|---|---|
| 1. | Army Transport Base | 25% | 16. | Hiroshima RR Station | 100% |
| 2. | Army Ordnance Depot | | 17. | Railroad Station U/E | 100% |
| 3. | Army Food Depot | 35% | 18. | Bridge,debris loaded,inta |
| 4. | Army Clothing Depot | 85% | 19. | Bridge, 1/4 missing |
| 5. | E.Hiroshima RR Station | 30% | 20. | Large bridge,shattered, " |
| 6. | U/E industry | 90% | 21. | Bridge,large hole W. side |
| 7. | Sumitomo Rayon Plant | 25% | 22. | Bridge,intact,banks caved |
| 8. | Kinkwa Rayon Mill | 10% | 23. | Bridge, " debris covered |
| 9. | Teikoku Textile Mill | 100% | 24. | Both bridges intact |
| 10. | Power Plant | ? | 25. | Bridge, 100% destroyed |
| 11. | Oil Storage | On fire | 26. | Bridge,severely damaged |
| 12. | Elec.Ry Power Sta | 100% | 27. | Bridge, destroyed |
| 13. | Elec.Power Generator | 100% | 28. | Bridge,shattered,inoperati |
| 14. | Telephone Company | 100% | 29. | Bridge,intact,slight damage |
| 15. | Hiroshima Gas Works | 100% | 30. | Bridge,intact,severely dma |

( 8:16 A.M. ) When Little Boy had dropped to 1,902 feet (580 m) above Hiroshima, a radar signal bounced off the ground to trigger the bomb's third and final switch. The bomb exploded.

The crew of the Enola Gay had no idea what an atomic explosion would look like. A dazzling purple flash suddenly lit up the inside of their plane. The co-pilot Lewis believed he could taste lead. Although they were 12.4 miles (20 km) from the blast, shock waves rocked the plane so violently that Tibbets thought they were being hit by antiaircraft fire. Staring back to where Hiroshima had stood moments before, the crew saw a monstrous vision of searing flame and swirling smoke devouring the city. They grasped for familiar images to understand the unreal scene before them. Navigator Theodore Van Kirk wrote that the city looked like a pot of boiling, black oil. Radar expert Jacob Beser said, "Did you ever go to the beach and stir up the sand in shallow water and see it all billow up? That's what it looked like to me."

The voice of Sergeant George Caron, the B-29's tail-gunner, was recorded on tape as he narrated the destruction of Hiroshima: "A bubbling mass, purple-gray in color, with that red core. It's all turbulent. Fires are springing up everywhere, like flames shooting out of a huge bed of coals.... Here it comes, the mushroom shape.... It's like a mass of bubbling molasses.... It's growing up and up and up. It's nearly level with us and climbing.... The city must be below that."

# August 6, 1945: Stopping the Clocks

The hands of this wristwatch recovered from Hiroshima were fixed forever at 8.16 by the heat of the blast.

8:16 A.M. | Clocks and watches found in the ashes of Hiroshima had all stopped at 8:16 A.M., their hands forever displaying this moment in time. At this instant, the atomic bomb's searing heat scorched the surfaces of buildings, and printed these surfaces with the permanent shadows of people standing against them. Those few buildings

that were not flattened leaned sideways as if shying from the blast. Bridges over the river buckled upward as massive shock waves bounced off the water. Railway tracks curled and twisted, and steel pylons swayed like trees in a gale.

Ground Zero | The bomb exploded some 820 feet (250 m) off target. The point directly beneath the blast, known as Ground Zero, was not the Aioi Bridge but a private hospital. The hospital simply vanished, leaving nothing but a few concrete pillars driven into the ground like giant nails. A flash of unimaginably intense heat and light, lasting a fraction of a second, heated the earth to nearly 3,000 °C. In the sky, birds and insects caught fire. More than 3,000 people within 1,640 feet (500 m) of Ground Zero were killed instantly—their shriveled corpses left standing like statues of black wood. The fingertips of some glowed with strange blue flames.

.3 mile | People more than one-third mile (500 m) away from the blast survived long enough to see a flash so bright that many of them were blinded. The flash was followed by a blossoming orange fireball, which seared their clothes and flesh with an overwhelming heat as it rolled over them. Granite walls and clay roof tiles melted, and skin ran from people's bodies like wax. A massive shock-wave flattened buildings with a force as powerful as that of the tsunami (tidal waves) that sometimes struck the coastline of Japan. It tore from people their tattered shreds of burned clothing, skin, and hair.

1.2 miles | At this distance, every wooden building burst into flames and people suffered blistering burns unlike anything seen before. Women who had been wearing white kimonos with patterns of dark flowers had those flowers seared into their skin like tattoos. The blast turned buildings to rubble, then stirred up a deadly tornado of broken glass and hurled people into its heart.

**7.5 miles** Unlike people in the downtown, for whom the dazzling flash was strangely silent, those further away heard a roar so loud they thought an ammunition dump had exploded. Every window or mirror facing the blast was shattered.

Hiroshima had a population of about a quarter of a million civilians and 43,000 soldiers. More than 80,000 of them were killed at 8:16 A.M. on August 6, 1945, and tens of thousands more would die in the coming hours, days, and years.

A photograph of Hiroshima taken in 1946 shows how completely the city was destroyed by the atomic bomb.

## A Moment in Time

Almost one mile away from Ground Zero, the Red Cross Hospital collapses. Dr Sasaki's slippers are ripped from his feet, but he is miraculously unhurt. He is one of the lucky ones—65 of Hiroshima's 150 doctors are now dead. About three-fourths of a mile from Ground Zero, 5-year-old Myeko and her family are buried beneath the rubble of their house—but they too will survive the blast. Three-fifths of a mile from Ground Zero, the schoolgirl, the soldier, and the prisoner of war are incinerated. Thousands of people around them suffer the same fate.

## Hell on Earth

" It was just like hell—a procession of ghosts, a sea of flames. But I did not see the devil, so I thought it was something happening on this earth. "

*A survivor.*

Victims wait to receive first aid in the southern part of Hiroshima a few hours after the atomic blast on August 6, 1945.

SMOKE AND ASH BLOSSOMED into a mushroom-shaped cloud that towered an astonishing 7.5 miles (12 km) above Hiroshima. This cloud plunged what was left of the city into darkness. Survivors, who could not begin to understand what had just happened, found themselves in a flat, black, burning wasteland. Hiroshima had ceased to exist. A schoolboy: "We found a world such as I had never seen before, a world I'd never even heard of before. I saw human bodies in such a state that you couldn't tell whether they were humans." A soldier: "When I came to my senses, I found my comrades still standing erect and saluting; when I said 'Hey,' and tapped their shoulders, they crumbled down into ashes."

Among the general horror, there were images that survivors would always carry with them—a dead man still astride his bicycle; carp swimming among corpses in a pond; a swallow with burned wings hopping about; a terribly burned man rolling on the ground and pleading, "Will somebody please kill me!"

Crowds of survivors stumbled like sleepwalkers, silent as ghosts. Most were naked, blackened by ash and blood. They held their burned arms out to stop them touching their burned bodies. Many had lost their hair; on the heads of others it stood up straight from the shock. All suffered an unbearable thirst. To quench this, and to escape the raging flames,

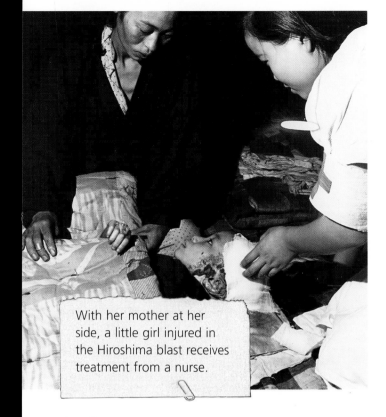

With her mother at her side, a little girl injured in the Hiroshima blast receives treatment from a nurse.

Steel girders in Hiroshima were twisted and buckled by the force of the atomic blast.

they flocked to the riverbanks. The crush became so great that hundreds were pressed into the water and silently drowned. Hiroshima's rivers soon became clogged with corpses.

At one point, four government officials pushed through the crowds crying, "The Emperor's picture!" Ignoring their injuries, people stepped aside, bowing low as the picture was carried past. A passing boat was summoned to the riverbank to transport the sacred portrait of Hirohito to safety.

Little Boy had not finished its work. As the hot air of the mushroom cloud cooled and condensed, a shower of enormous, black, sticky, radioactive raindrops tumbled down on the city. The raindrops left gray marks on people's skin. Rivers turned black as ink, and dead fish floated to the surface.

Fifty-two of Hiroshima's 55 hospitals had been destroyed. Emergency aid stations were set up, but most of the nurses had died in the blast and medical supplies were even scarcer than before the bomb's arrival. What help could there be for the survivors?

## A Moment in Time

At 2:58 P.M., as the firestorm rages through Hiroshima, the Enola Gay lands at North Field. A huge crowd has gathered for a welcome party. As Tibbets leaves the plane, a general steps forward and pins the Distinguished Service Cross onto his chest. At the same moment, President Truman is enjoying lunch on the cruiser *Augusta* on his voyage home from Potsdam. Hearing news of the bomb's success, he tells fellow diners: "This is the greatest thing in history."

The Japanese set up relief stations near the cities of Hiroshima and Nagasaki, where victims of the atomic attacks could receive treatment.

ON AUGUST 6, A MESSAGE was broadcast from the White House to Japan: "The force from which the Sun draws its power has been loosed upon those who brought war to the Far East....It was to spare the Japanese people from utter destruction that the ultimatum of July 26 was issued at Potsdam. Their leaders promptly rejected that ultimatum. If they do not now accept our terms they may expect a rain of ruin from the air, the like of which has never been seen on this earth."

But the Potsdam announcement had given no warning of an atomic bomb. It was difficult even now for the Japanese to understand that their enemy suddenly possessed a weapon of such overwhelming power. Hiroshima's communications had been destroyed so completely that accurate news of the attack could not be sent. Even when reports of the explosion were received, they were dismissed as wild exaggerations.

When Lieutenant-General Seizo Arisue flew to Hiroshima to assess the damage, he discovered the reality. There were so few landmarks left that his pilot had trouble navigating. Arisue stepped from the plane into an eerie, silent stillness. The officer who welcomed him revealed: "Not my daughter alone, but thousands of other innocent children were massacred. This new bomb is satanic, too atrocious and horrible to use."

In Washington, some of the American leaders had reached the same conclusion. Studying photographs of Hiroshima's devastation, they expressed revulsion that their country could use such an "inhuman" weapon. But without Japan's unconditional surrender, Truman was determined to launch a second attack.

Events collided on the morning of August 9, 1945. At the same moment as Soviet troops were invading Japanese-held Manchuria (a region in the northeast of China), Major Charles Sweeney took off from North Field in a B-29 bomber named Bock's Car. It was loaded with a Fat Man plutonium bomb like the one tested at Alamogordo. Six hours later, Bock's Car began its bombing run over the Japanese city of Kokura, but found the target obscured by smoke. So a different city became the second to be obliterated by an atomic bomb. At 11.01 A.M., the Fat Man was dropped on the port of Nagasaki. The people of Hiroshima would not be alone in their horror. Japanese ministers meeting at 11:00 A.M. that morning still had their heads in the clouds. Emperor Hirohito urged surrender, but War Minister General Korechika Anami demanded that the Japanese must fight a last, glorious battle to defend their homeland. As the Fat Man descended on Nagasaki, he was asking colleagues: "Who can be 100 percent sure of defeat?"

## American Views

" I regarded the bomb as a military weapon, and never had any doubt that it should be used. "

*Harry S. Truman, U.S. President 1945–1952.*

" My own feeling was that in being the first to use it we had adopted the ethical standards common to barbarians in the Dark Ages. "

*Admiral William D. Leahy, U.S. Chief of Staff, 1942–1949.*

The bomb dropped on Nagasaki was a "Fat Man" plutonium bomb like this one. It was almost 10 feet (3 m) long and weighed more than four tons.

A Japanese delegation led by Foreign Minister Mamoru Shigemitsu (in top hat) and Army Chief of Staff Yoshijiro Umezu (in uniform) watches as General MacArthur leans forward to add his signature to the Japanese surrender document.

JUST AS THE JAPANESE people seemed on the edge of destruction by a bomb of supernatural force, so a figure they believed to be supernatural—Emperor Hirohito—intervened to end their terrible suffering.

Many ministers believed that the atomic bomb attacks offered the perfect opportunity to surrender without loss of honor. But the generals of Japan—a nation that had never known defeat—vowed to fight on, and War Minister Anami blocked all suggestions of surrender.

At last, both the deadlock and Japanese tradition were broken when the members of the Cabinet were summoned to Hirohito's air-raid shelter. The emperor was a little man with thick spectacles, but he was held to be so sacred that the politicians did not dare to look directly at him. Hirohito was not supposed to interfere in worldly matters, but now he expressed his wishes: "The time has come when we must bear the unbearable. I swallow my tears and give my sanction to the proposal to accept the Allied proclamation."

In the following days, Japanese and American officials negotiated terms. Even after suffering the devastation of two atomic bombs, the Japanese insisted that the emperor's status be guaranteed. A compromise was reached, with the Americans proposing that a new government in Japan would "be established by the freely expressed will of the Japanese people."

However, within Japan there was resistance to the decision to surrender. Events came to a head on August 15, 1945. In the early hours, rebellious officers took over the royal palace but failed to win support for a military coup. Realizing that all was lost, Anami plunged a dagger into his stomach, committing the ritual suicide of seppuku. At midday, a scratchy phonograph recording of the emperor's surrender speech, which Hirohito had made the previous evening, was broadcast throughout Japan. For millions of people who had never before heard their divine emperor's voice, it was a moment of both joy and despair. Outside the royal palace in Tokyo, amid weeping crowds, military officers shot themselves rather than face surrender.

In Washington the announcement of the war's end unleashed wild celebrations. Two million Americans gathered in Times Square in New York, fireworks lit up Pearl Harbor, and the Los Alamos scientists fired a 21-gun salute of high explosives.

On September 2, 1945, eleven Japanese delegates—some dressed in military uniform, others in top hats and tails—were piped aboard the USS *Missouri* anchored in Tokyo Bay. Watched by crowds that included American prisoners of war who were so thin that they resembled skeletons, Supreme Allied Commander General Douglas MacArthur accepted Japan's written surrender.

## A Moment in Time

At noon on August 15, 1945, the survivors at Hiroshima gather around a loudspeaker set up amid the ruins of the railway station. The national anthem, *Reign of Our Emperor*, crackles through the speaker before, wonder of wonders, they hear the voice of the emperor himself. Here, of all places, people understand what Hirohito means when he explains how the use of "a new and most cruel bomb" has forced Japan's surrender. Yet, confused by the emperor's formal language and their own unshakable faith in victory, some at the station insist that Japan has won the war.

Japanese prisoners of war bow their heads as they listen to Emperor Hirohito announce that the time has come for Japan to surrender.

33

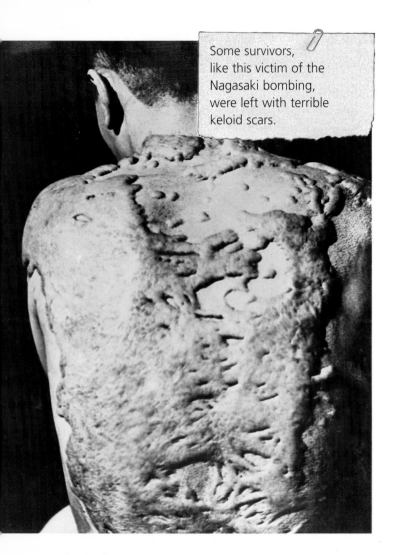

Some survivors, like this victim of the Nagasaki bombing, were left with terrible keloid scars.

THE SURVIVORS OF HIROSHIMA were the first people ever to live through the effects of an atomic bomb. A new vocabulary came into being to describe the traumatic events, including words like *pika-don*—for a lightning flash and a loud boom—and *hibakusha*—for explosion-affected persons. Just as there were no words, so there was no history to help the people of Hiroshima understand their suffering.

The city of Hiroshima was not evacuated after the bombing. Instead, the hibakusha returned to the rubble to rebuild their homes. In the following weeks, many became sick, and began to cough blood. Their hair fell out in clumps, and purple specks appeared on their skin. Those that were not ill lived in constant dread of

becoming so. One survivor wrote, "We were being killed against our will by something unknown to us."

Without words, without history, the hibakusha could not know that Hiroshima was cloaked in an invisible cloud of lethal radiation. The aftereffects of Little Boy continued to kill at random, and by 1950 the deaths resulting from the bombing had risen to some 200,000. The radiation also caused cancer, which would continue to claim lives for decades.

Although the emperor remained on his throne, between 1945 and 1952 an Allied occupation force governed Japan. The silence that had fallen over Hiroshima on the day of the bombing now became compulsory, as the Allies censored all references to the atom bomb—including the sketchbooks that the hibakusha had made of their experiences.

For ten years, Hiroshima received no government help. In September 1956, the Japanese Red Cross Society used lottery funds to build the Hiroshima A-bomb Hospital. Twenty-five women whose burns had developed disfiguring growths known as keloid scars were invited to the United States to undergo plastic surgery. In 1957, a relief law was passed, and the hibakusha at last received allowances and free medical treatment.

## A Survivor's Voice

" People were dying so fast that I had begun to accept death as a matter of course and ceased to respect its awfulness. I considered a family lucky if it had not lost more than two of its members. "

*Dr. Michihiko Hachiya, who survived the bombing and treated people suffering from radiation poisoning.*

In 1955, the Peace Memorial Park opened in Hiroshima. The point beneath which the bomb had exploded was marked with a clay arch like those found in ancient Japanese tombs. On August 6 every year, people still gather there and float colored lanterns down the river in a Buddhist ceremony to remember the dead. Some hibakusha marked the anniversaries by calling for peace and speaking out against atomic weapons. But many had found their own peace in silence. Some commemorated the 30th anniversary of the attack on Hiroshima by drawing pictures of the bombing, but one of them said, "Even if I drew a hundred pictures, they could not tell you of my experiences."

Hiroshima survivors join a peace march in 1962.

Life goes on in Hiroshima, but the shattered Gengaku Dome has been preserved as a permanent reminder of the damage done by the atomic bomb.

WHAT IF, ON AUGUST 6, 1945, the attack on Hiroshima had not taken place? People who support the use of the atomic bomb at Hiroshima tend to focus on this question. They argue that the war might have continued with the loss of even more lives. But even if this is true, does it justify the use of such a weapon?

**If the bomb had not been dropped:**

...the United States would have invaded Japan on November 1, 1945. At Potsdam, Army Chief of Staff General George Marshall warned President Truman that an invasion would cost more than 250,000 American lives. Japanese losses would have been far greater. If the invasion had gone ahead, Japanese officers would have followed orders to kill prisoners of war. By this point in history, most of the world was desperate to end, by any means, a conflict that had already cost an estimated 55 million lives.

...Curtis LeMay's B-29s would have bombed Hiroshima with incendiaries. LeMay admitted that if Japan had won the conflict, he would have been tried as a war criminal for the use of incendiaries against Tokyo's civilians. Hiroshima raised even greater moral questions. Little Boy was a weapon capable of terrible destruction, with effects similar to those of chemical warfare. And the scientists at Los Alamos were certainly aware of some of the dangers of radiation.

Japanese defendants at a war crimes trial in Tokyo in 1946. Seven of Japan's leaders, including wartime prime minister General Tojo, were hanged for their part in atrocities.

Curtis LeMay, left, plans his bombing campaign in May 1945. LeMay stated that, had Japan won the war, he would have been tried as a war criminal.

## Viewpoints

" If the A-bomb had not been dropped, we would have had great difficulty to find a good reason to end the war. "

*Hisatune Sakomizu, secretary to the Japanese Cabinet.*

" When the bombs dropped and news began to circulate that... we would not be obliged to run up the beaches near Tokyo... while being mortared and shelled... we cried with relief and joy. We were going to live. We were going to grow up to adulthood after all. "

*Paul Fussell, a 21-year-old American second-lieutenant.*

" The Japanese were ready to surrender, and it wasn't necessary to hit them with that awful thing. "

*General Dwight D. Eisenhower.*

...the Japanese might have starved. A naval blockade had halted all supplies, and by July 1945 Japan's government was instructing its people to eat acorns. An American survey conducted after the war showed that the Japanese faced starvation by November 1945. Some writers have argued that using the atomic bomb to subdue war-ravaged Japan was like murdering a man already on his deathbed.

...Japan might have dropped its own bomb. In fact, the Japanese did not have sufficient resources to build an atomic bomb, but it is interesting to note that throughout the war, physicist Yoshio Nishina was conducting atomic bomb experiments at a Tokyo laboratory.

...a surrender might have been negotiated. Even after Hiroshima, Japan surrendered only when the emperor's position was guaranteed. If the United States had agreed to this at Potsdam, the war might have ended sooner. Secretary of War Henry Stimson wrote, "History might find that the United States, in its delay in stating its position on unconditional surrender terms, had prolonged the war."

...the Soviet Union would have invaded Japan. This was one reason why President Truman wanted to end the war quickly. The Americans were afraid that the Soviets might steal their victory. Some historians argue that the bomb was dropped not only to defeat Japan, but also to demonstrate the United States' new military power to the Soviet Union, and give the Americans the upper hand in their post-war rivalry.

A mushroom cloud rises from the first superbomb test in the Marshall Islands in 1952.

IN 1946, THE AMERICAN navy removed the inhabitants from Bikini Atoll in the Pacific's remote Marshall Islands. The islanders sang as they departed, having been told that God would be pleased, and they could soon return. On July 1, 1946, a B-29 called Dave's Dream dropped an atomic bomb on target ships anchored in the atoll. Radiation remained poorly understood; hours after the test, American sailors scrubbed down the battered target ships and had their lunch on board. During the next 12 years, the United States would unleash 23 massive explosions at Bikini to study the effects of nuclear bombs.

However, the American monopoly on the atomic bomb did not last long. Truman had first told the Soviets of the new weapon at Potsdam, but Stalin had reacted so casually that Truman thought he did not understand what he was saying. In fact, Stalin understood very well. Klaus Fuchs, one of the scientists who had escaped from Germany to join the Manhattan Project, had been passing its secrets to the Soviets. On August 29, 1949, scientists led by Igor Kurchatov gathered in northeast Kazakhstan for a test called First Lightning. At 7:00 A.M., they exploded Joe 1, a plutonium bomb just like the Fat Man. There were now two atomic superpowers.

Mutual fear and mistrust between the United States and the Soviet Union started a perilous race to build weapons of ever-greater destruction. Scientists at Los Alamos developed a superbomb that worked not by splitting atoms but by joining them together. This "fusion" of hydrogen atoms at extremely high temperatures created an explosion of limitless devastation. Some scientists, such as Oppenheimer, opposed the superbomb as "a danger to humanity." Others, led by the Hungarian Edward Teller, worked to develop it ahead of the Soviets.

On November 1, 1952, the superbomb was detonated on Enewetak Atoll in the Marshall Islands. Little Boy had weighed four tons. This monster weighed over 80. Its fireball grew to 3.1 miles (5 km) across, its mushroom cloud spread 99.4 miles (160 km) wide. The island beneath the bomb vanished, and 80 million tons of radioactive earth were sucked up into the atmosphere. Fish were found 2.5 miles (4 km) away with their skin burned off. The superbomb had unleashed the devastation of 1,000 Hiroshimas.

The science that had ended the war was now threatening to end the world. In 1961, the atomic rivalry culminated in the Soviet Union detonating the world's largest superbomb on an island in the Arctic Ocean. By 1963, tests had increased the radiation in the world's atmosphere by 7 percent. Even today, Bikini Atoll remains too radioactive for the islanders to return home.

## A Moment in Time

On March 1, 1954, 23 Japanese fishermen on the *Lucky Dragon No. 5* are fishing in the Pacific. At the same moment, 81 miles (130 km) away, American scientists gather once more at Bikini Atoll. They are testing Bravo, a new type of hydrogen bomb. They unleash an explosion 1,500 times more powerful than the Hiroshima bomb. Coral is sucked into the atmosphere, and radioactive ash is scattered over 32,000 square miles (80,000 sq km). The fishermen watch this fatal snow flutter down. The ash also falls on Rongelap Atoll, where children play with it and taste it.

When *Lucky Dragon No. 5* returns to port two weeks later, its fishermen are ill. One will die from radiation poisoning. On Rongelap, three out of four young children will develop tumors. The American Atomic Energy Commission insists that the Bravo test was not out of control.

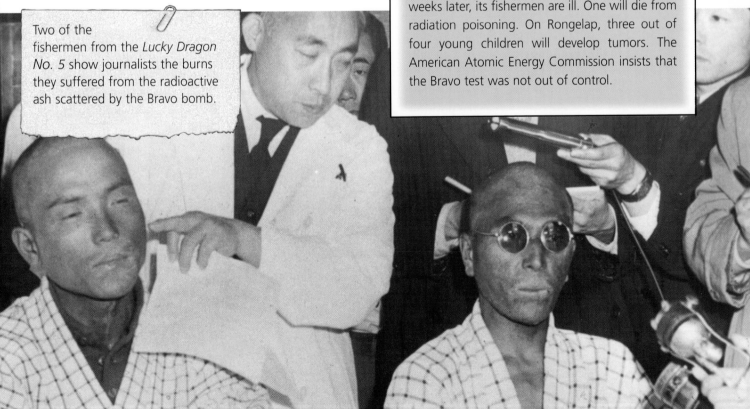

Two of the fishermen from the *Lucky Dragon No. 5* show journalists the burns they suffered from the radioactive ash scattered by the Bravo bomb.

President Kennedy (left) and General Thomas Powers, beside the phone which would be used to order an atomic attack. Powers once said: "At the end of the war, if there are two Americans and one Russian left alive, we win."

THE MUSHROOM CLOUD THAT blossomed over Hiroshima cast a terrible shadow over the future of the world. As they made their brutal firework displays of nuclear power, the Soviet Union and the United States discovered that the position they were in was deeply ironic. Their weapons of war had become too powerful to use. So, they were reduced to threat and counterthreat, bluff and double-bluff. Their behavior, in what became known as the Cold War, was like that of two heavyweight boxers flexing their muscles but never daring to throw a punch.

In 1954, American Secretary of State John Foster Dulles created the American policy of massive retaliation. He made it clear that any Communist expansion in Europe would be met with a colossal nuclear strike against the Soviet Union. In 1957, the superpowers tested their first ICBMs (Inter-Continental Ballistic Missiles), which could deliver nuclear warheads across the globe. The two heavyweights now stood eye to eye, and the arms race gathered pace.

The perilous standoff came to a head on a little island in the Caribbean. On October 14, 1962, American U-2 spy planes photographed atomic missile sites on Cuba. This island lay only 93 miles (150 km) from Florida and was ruled by the communist regime of Fidel Castro. The Soviet leader, Nikita Khrushchev, had sent troops and missiles to Cuba in response to the deployment of American missiles in Turkey. The young American president, John F. Kennedy, gave a live television broadcast to announce the crisis. He ordered a naval blockade of Cuba, and American pilots began flying with the safety devices removed from their atomic bombs.

On October 27, 1962—known as Black Saturday—people genuinely believed the world was about to end. The United States made plans to invade Cuba, and the Soviets prepared to respond by launching nuclear missiles 75 times more powerful than Little Boy. When the Cubans shot down an American spy plane, generals including Curtis LeMay demanded retaliation. Realizing that the world was on the verge of nuclear war, President Kennedy overruled them. After frantic negotiations, he made a secret deal with Khrushchev.

Kennedy and his generals under the shadow of U.S. nuclear missiles during the Cuban Missile Crisis.

Missiles would be removed from both Turkey and Cuba. The crisis was over.

Kennedy later said that he had found himself trapped between the national suicide of massive retaliation and the national humiliation of conceding to the Soviets. Hiroshima had resulted in a world armed with the weapons of its own destruction and teetering on the brink of nuclear war. But perhaps the very memories of Hiroshima, the images of the horrific effects of the atomic bomb, had helped the crisis to end in peace.

## The Cuban Missile Crisis

" It was a beautiful fall evening, the height of the crisis, and I went up into the open air to look and to smell it, because I thought it was the last Saturday I would ever see. "

*U.S. Secretary for Defense Robert McNamara, on the evening of Saturday, October 27, 1962.*

" That was when I went and telephoned my wife and told her to drop everything and get out of Moscow. I thought then that the American bombers were on their way. "

*Fyodor Burlatsky, Soviet journalist, on the same day.*

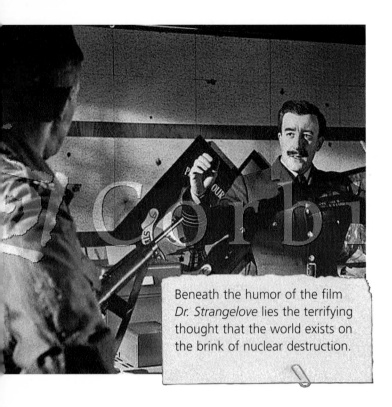

Beneath the humor of the film *Dr. Strangelove* lies the terrifying thought that the world exists on the brink of nuclear destruction.

THE DAY AN ATOMIC bomb exploded over Hiroshima left a legacy that fundamentally changed the world. The splitting of the atom also split apart the very meanings of war and peace. It led to the age of the Cold War, where the brooding presence of nuclear weapons simultaneously secured an armed peace and threatened the world with annihilation. Nuclear strategist Albert Wohlstetter famously called this a "delicate balance of terror."

The scientists at Los Alamos were aware that their creation was a double-edged sword. In May 1945, Leo Szilard carried another letter from Einstein to the president—this time to argue that the bomb was simply too devastating to use. When leading politicians and scientists met that same month, Secretary of War Henry Stimson noted of the atomic bomb, "May destroy or perfect international civilization.... Frankenstein, or means for world peace."

This legacy of a Frankenstein's monster marshaling the peace became known, appropriately, as MAD (Mutually Assured Destruction). Both the United States and the Soviet Union based their nuclear defenses on the ability to strike back against their enemy's first strike. In this way, neither could launch an attack without inviting its own destruction. This MAD deterrent has not prevented a succession of wars using conventional weapons, but Little Boy and the Fat Man remain the only two atomic bombs ever to have been used in war.

For ordinary people, the legacy of Hiroshima was overwhelming. Throughout the Cold War, as fallout shelters were built and children practiced drills for surviving a nuclear holocaust, people confronted the very real fear that civilization might end. This fear, reinforced by the images of Hiroshima, led to the peace movements of the 1960s that awakened an interest in protest and politics among a new generation. But the success of the peace movement has been limited—it has been estimated that in the fifty years after the bombing of Hiroshima, the world spent $8 billion on weapons.

The atomic bomb also created a cultural legacy. This ranges from the instantly recognizable symbol of CND (Campaign for Nuclear Disarmament) to films such as Stanley Kubrick's *Dr. Strangelove or How I Learned to Stop Worrying and Love the Bomb*. This satire's theme of a mad political leader starting a nuclear war remains terrifyingly relevant today. Britain, France, and China have joined the United States and the Soviet Union as nuclear powers, and in the 1990s both India and Pakistan tested nuclear weapons. The possibility of a nuclear threat being developed by a smaller nation with a fanatical leader poses a genuine challenge to world peace.

Japan regained its independence in 1952, the same year that the United States tested the first superbomb. Today the two countries have close links and both are industrial powers. Hiroshima now has a population of over one million. It is an example of civilization's ability to rebuild. But this should not overshadow the lasting legacy of Hiroshima as a monument to humankind's capacity for destruction.

## A Monstrous Power

" I shuddered to think that future ages might curse me as their pest, whose selfishness had not hesitated to buy its own peace at the price, perhaps, of the existence of the whole human race. "

*Mary Shelley, from her novel* Frankenstein, 1818.

" A new thing had just been born; a new control; a new understanding of man, which man had acquired over nature. "

*Isidor Rabi, American physicist at the Trinity test, July 16, 1945.*

A child sets a lantern afloat at the Peace Memorial Park in Hiroshima on August 6, 2000, exactly 55 years after the city was destroyed.

# Glossary

**Allies**  The Allies were the nations that fought against Germany, Italy, and Japan in World War II. The Allies included Great Britain, the United States, the Soviet Union, and China, and totaled 50 nations by the end of the war.

**atoll**  A ring of coral islands enclosing a lagoon.

**atom**  The smallest particle of an element, which consists of electrons surrounding a central nucleus containing protons and neutrons.

**atomic**  Having to do with atoms, or producing energy from atoms.

**atomic pile**  An atomic reactor.

**atomic reactor**  A device which splits atoms to create a controlled chain reaction that releases energy without causing an explosion.

**banzai**  Both a Japanese greeting, and the war cry used by Japanese soldiers when making suicidal charges.

**Burma–Thailand Railway**  The railway built to carry supplies from Thailand to Japanese troops fighting in Burma. It was constructed by 61,000 Allied prisoners of war and 270,000 native laborers pressed into service by the Japanese. Many of the laborers died under dreadful conditions.

**Bushido**  The code followed by Samurai warriors in ancient Japan, and adopted by Japanese soldiers in World War II. Death was preferred to capture, and suicide was preferred to surrender, which was considered a disgrace.

**condensed**  Changed from a gas or vapor into a liquid.

**coup**  An abbreviation of *coup d'état*, meaning a sudden act that brings down a government, usually through military force.

**firestorm**  A terrible fire, such as that created by an atomic explosion, where the flames create a gale that fans the flames and increases the fire.

**fission**  The splitting of an atom by bombarding the nucleus with neutrons.

***Frankenstein***  The title of a novel by Mary Shelley. The word has come to have three meanings: a scientist who creates a monster he cannot control; the monster itself; or anything that can destroy its creator.

**fusion**  The combining of the nuclei of two atoms at extremely high temperatures, releasing huge amounts of energy.

**Geneva Convention**  An international agreement signed in 1929, providing for the humane treatment of prisoners, civilians, and the wounded in times of war. The Allies informed Japan that it would observe the Convention. Japan had signed the agreement, but insisted that it had not been ratified by its government, and Japanese officers largely ignored it.

**incendiary bombs**  Bombs containing substances such as napalm that start fires when they explode.

**infamy**  Disgrace and negative fame arising from acts of evil.

**isotope**  One of two or more forms of a chemical element, having the same chemical properties but a different atomic weight and different physical properties. U-235 is an isotope of uranium.

**kamikazes**  In 1281, Japan was saved from invasion when gales sunk the fleet of the Mongol warlord Kublai Khan. Thanking their gods, the Japanese called the gales "Kamikaze," meaning "Divine Wind." During World War II this name was given to suicide pilots.

**monopoly**  When one person, company, or country has exclusive control or possession of something. The United States enjoyed a monopoly on the atomic bomb until the Soviet Union developed one.

**Nazi Germany**  Germany under the control of the National Socialist Party, which came to power in 1933 under the dictator Adolf Hitler, who led Germany into World War II.

**neutrons** Tiny particles that form part of the nucleus of atoms.

**nuclear** Another word for atomic.

**phonograph** An old type of record player.

**plutonium** A radioactive metallic element that can be produced from uranium, and is used to create atomic energy.

**radar** RAdio Detection And Ranging. The system used for determining the distance, speed, and direction of unseen objects by bouncing radio waves off them.

**radiation** Rays and particles released by the disintegration of atoms. The radiation released by an atomic bomb is extremely harmful and long-lasting.

**radioactive** Giving off radiation and energy through the breaking up of atoms.

**raw materials** Substances in their natural states, such as the products of mines and farms, and including such things as rubber, oil, coal, and iron ore.

**Samurai** The famous class of skilled and disciplined warriors of Japanese society, who since 1100 followed a rigid code of honor.

**seppuku** Also called *hara-kiri*, a ritual and very painful form of suicide practiced in Japan, and committed by drawing a knife across the abdomen.

**U-235** An isotope contained in uranium, which can be produced by splitting uranium atoms and is a source of atomic energy.

**uranium** A radioactive, metallic, chemical element, the heaviest natural element, containing isotopes that can be used as a source of atomic energy.

# Further Information

## Reading

Black, Wallace B. *Hiroshima and the Atomic Bomb*. Parsippany, NJ: Silver Burdett Press, 1992.

Farris, John. *Hiroshima*. Farmington Hills, MI: Gale Group, 1990.

Feinberg, Barbara Silberdick. *Hiroshima and Nagasaki*. New York: Children's Press, 1995.

Grant, R. G. *Hiroshima and Nagasaki (New Perspectives)*. New York: Raintree Steck-Vaughn Publishers, 1998.

Sherrow, Victoria. *Hiroshima*. Parsippany, NJ: Silver Burdett Press, 1994.

Tames, Richard. *Hiroshima: The Shadow of the Bomb (Point of Impact)*. Chicago, IL: Heinemann Library, 2001.

Yep, Laurence. *Hiroshima: A Novella*. New York: Scholastic, 1996.

Young, Robert. *Hiroshima: Fifty Years of Debate*. Parsippany, NJ: Silver Burdett Press, 1994.

Ziff, John. *The Bombing of Hiroshima (Great Disasters: Reforms and Ramifications)*. Broomall, PA: Chelsea House Publishers, 2001.

## Films

*Hiroshima* directed by Koreyoshi Kurahara and Roger Spottiswoode (1995).

*Hiroshima: Out of the Ashes* directed by Peter Werner (1990).

*Hiroshima—Erinnern und Verdrangen* directed by Erwin Leiser (1986).

*ABC News: Lifting the Fog—The Bombing of Hiroshima and Nagasaki* directed by Allan Siegel (1991).

# Time Line

1905  Scientist Albert Einstein describes the energy contained within atoms.

1933  Einstein emigrates to the United States.

July 1937  Japan invades China.

December 8, 1938  Scientist Otto Hahn splits an atom.

September 1, 1939  Nazi Germany invades Poland, triggering the start of World War II.

October 1939  Einstein warns President Roosevelt of the possibility of an atomic bomb.

July 1941  Japanese troops occupy French Indo-China.

December 7, 1941  Japanese bombers attack the U.S. Fleet at Pearl Harbor on Oahu, Hawaii. During the following week, the United States and Britain declare war on Japan, and the United States declares war on Germany and Italy.

1942  Japanese troops launch attacks in Southeast Asia.

June 1942  The Japanese fleet is defeated by the U.S. fleet at the Battle of Midway.

December 2, 1942  The world's first atomic reactor is tested in Chicago.

June 15, 1944  American B-29s fly from China to bomb Japan. U.S. troops land on Saipan in the Mariana Islands.

October 1944  The Japanese fleet is destroyed at the Battle of Leyte Gulf.

March 9, 1945  U.S. bombers set Tokyo ablaze in a "firestorm" raid.

April 1, 1945  U.S. troops land on Okinawa.

April 12, 1945  Harry Truman becomes U.S. president.

May 7, 1945  Nazi Germany surrenders to the Allies.

July 16, 1945  The world's first plutonium bomb is exploded in the Trinity test at Alamogordo, New Mexico.

July 26, 1945  The Allied leaders issue the Potsdam Proclamation, demanding Japan's surrender. The USS *Indianapolis* delivers the atomic bomb to Tinian.

August 6, 1945  The American bomber Enola Gay drops an atomic bomb on the Japanese city of Hiroshima.

August 9, 1945  Soviet troops invade Japanese-held Manchuria. The American bomber Bock's Car drops a plutonium bomb on the Japanese city of Nagasaki.

August 15, 1945  Japan surrenders.

September 2, 1945  Japanese officials sign surrender terms on board the USS *Missouri*.

July 1, 1946  The United States begins testing nuclear bombs at Bikini Atoll.

August 29, 1949  The Soviet Union explodes an atomic bomb in Kazakhstan.

1952  Japan regains its independence.

November 1, 1952  The United States explodes a hydrogen "superbomb" on Enewetak Atoll.

March 1, 1954  The United States stages the Bravo test on Bikini Atoll.

1955  The Peace Memorial Park opens in Hiroshima.

1956  The Hiroshima A-bomb Hospital is built.

1957  A law is passed in Japan giving relief funds to the survivors of the Hiroshima bombing.

October 1962  The Cuban Missile Crisis.

Frozen in time—the hands of a wristwatch recovered from Hiroshima.

# Index

© 2002 Hodder Wayland